# Note to parents, carers and teachers

*Read it yourself* is a series of modern stories, favourite characters, traditional tales and first reference books, written in a simple way for children who are learning to read. The books can be read independently or as part of a guided reading session.

Each book is carefully structured to include many high-frequency words vital for first reading. The sentences on each page are supported closely by pictures to help with understanding, and to offer lively details to talk about.

The books are graded into four levels that progressivel introduce wider vocabulary and longer text as a reader's ability and confidence grows.

## Ideas for use

- Although your child will now be progressing towards silent, independent reading, let her know that your help and encouragement is always available.

- Developing readers can be concentrating so hard on the words that they sometimes don't fully grasp the meaning of what they're reading. Answering the quiz questions at the end of the book will help with understanding.

*For more information and advice on Read it yourself and book banding, visit* **www.ladybird.com/readityourself**

Book Band 9

**Level 4** is ideal for children who are ready to read longer stories with a wider vocabulary and are eager to start reading independently.

# Special features:

Detailed illustrations capture the imagination

Full exploration of subject

Richer, more varied vocabulary

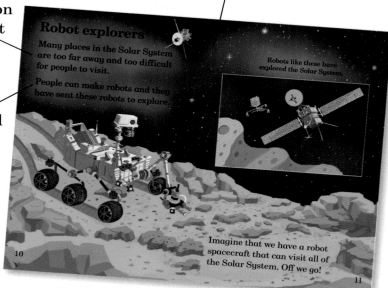

### Robot explorers

Many places in the Solar System are too far away and too difficult for people to visit.

People can make robots and they have sent these robots to explore.

Robots like these have explored the Solar System.

Imagine that we have a robot spacecraft that can visit all of the Solar System. Off we go!

10

11

Longer sentences

### Going to Mars

After Earth, we go on to Mars.

Mars is small and rocky and it has some ice. It is red because the rocks have rust in them.

robot explorer

moon

rust in rocks

Robot explorers from Earth have already been sent out to visit this red planet.

24    Mars         moon        25

Captions offer further explanation

Educational Consultant: Geraldine Taylor
Book Banding Consultant: Kate Ruttle
Subject Consultant: Dr Jacqueline Mitton

LADYBIRD BOOKS

UK | USA | Canada | Ireland | Australia
India | New Zealand | South Africa

Ladybird Books is part of the Penguin Random House group of companies
whose addresses can be found at global.penguinrandomhouse.com.

ladybird.com

Penguin
Random House
UK

First published 2016
001

Copyright © Ladybird Books Ltd, 2016
The moral right of the author and illustrator has been asserted

Printed in China

A CIP catalogue record for this book is available from the British Library

ISBN: 978–0–24123–741–0

# Our Solar System

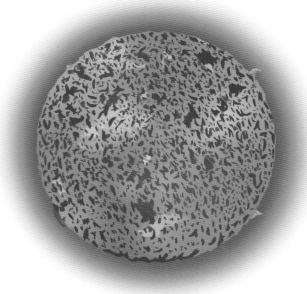

Written by Chris Baker
Illustrated by Ryan Wheatcroft

# Contents

# The Solar System

Our Solar System is huge.

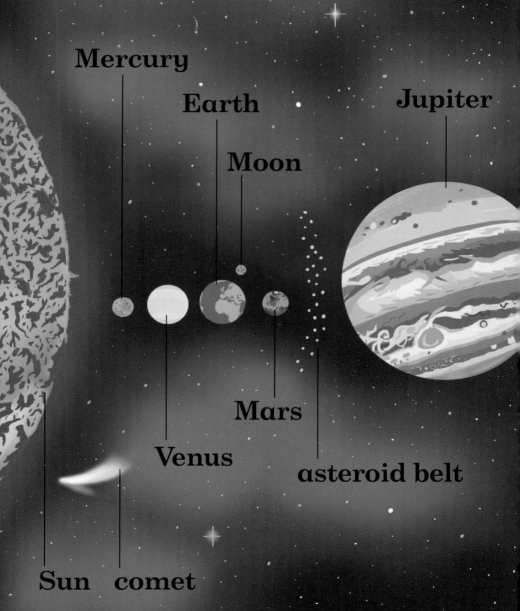

Mercury

Earth

Moon

Jupiter

Venus

Mars

asteroid belt

Sun   comet

It is difficult to imagine how massive it is.

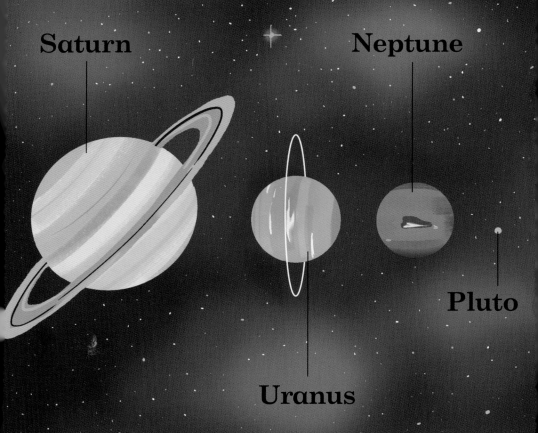

Saturn

Neptune

Uranus

Pluto

All these things are in our Solar System.

# Robot explorers

Many places in the Solar System are too far away and too difficult for people to visit.

People can make robots and they have sent these robots to explore.

Robots like these have explored the Solar System.

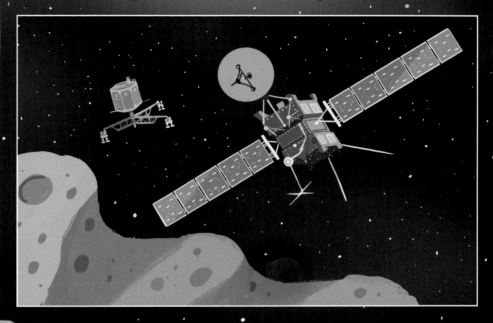

Imagine that we have a robot spacecraft that can visit all of the Solar System. Off we go!

# The Sun

The Sun makes the light and heat that people need to live on Earth.

The Sun is our nearest star and it is really huge. All the planets orbit (go around) the Sun.

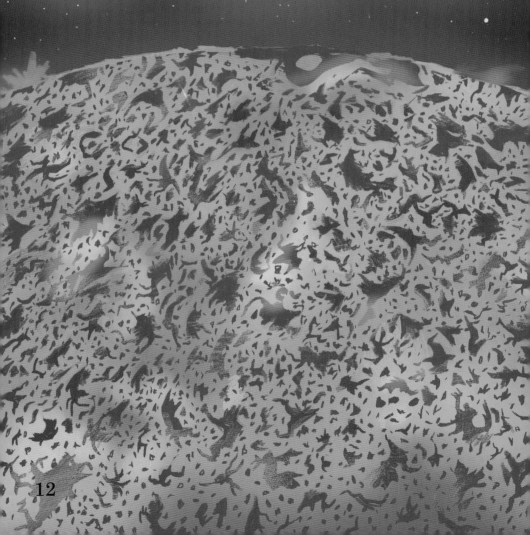

The Sun is the star in our
    Solar System.

# Mercury

We are coming to our first planet!
Mercury is next to the Sun.

The side near the Sun gets very hot
in the light, but the other side gets
really cold.

Mercury is a small, rocky planet near the Sun.

# Comets

Comets are chunks of rock
and ice that fly through the
Solar System.

tail

When ice from a comet comes off, it makes a big tail. It does this near the hot Sun.

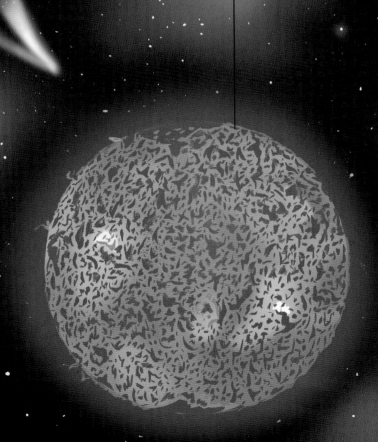

Sun

comet

# Going to Venus

Next stop, Venus!

Venus has thick clouds of acid all over. It is a very hot planet.

If we could look through these thick acid clouds, we would see a rocky planet.

# Planet Earth

Earth is the next planet to visit.

It is also the only planet where people can live. There is no water for them on other planets.

Earth ——————————————

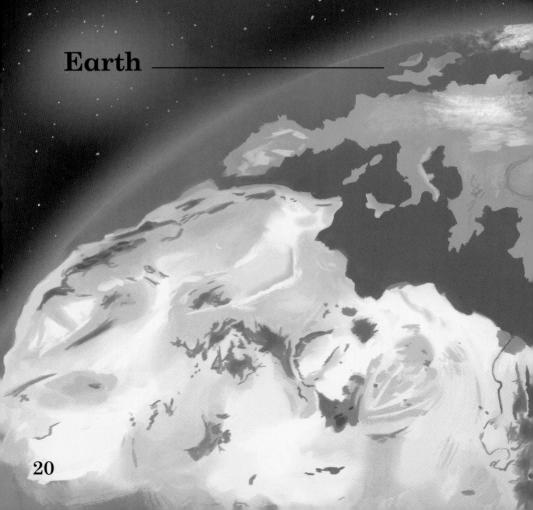

Earth is the only planet where there are all the things people need to live.

Moon

# Earth's Moon

Earth has a big moon. People have been here. It is rocky and has no water.

Earth ———— Moon

We can see some things that people used on the Moon before we go on to the next planet.

People went in a spacecraft to the Moon.

# Going to Mars

After the Moon, we go on to Mars.

Mars is small and rocky and it has some ice. It is red because the rocks have rust in them.

moon

Mars

moon

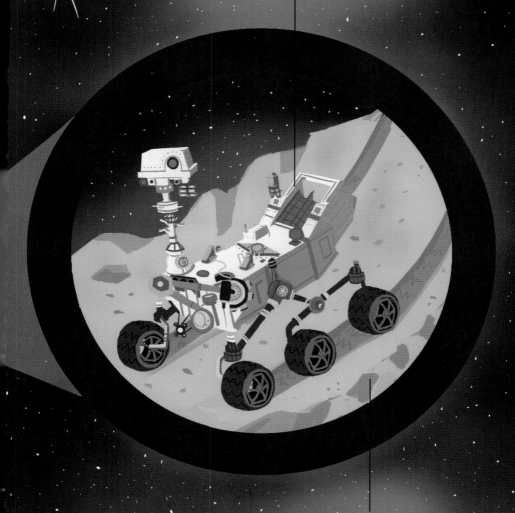

**robot explorer**

**rust in rocks**

Robot explorers from Earth have already
been sent out to visit this red planet.

# Asteroid belt

The asteroid belt is a ring of big and little chunks of rock.

They all orbit around the Sun.

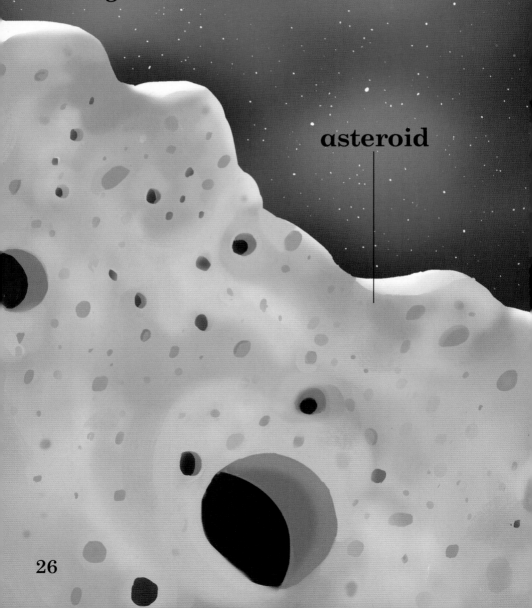

asteroid

The spacecraft is flying through the asteroid belt to the next planet.

# Jupiter

Our next stop is Jupiter.

Jupiter is the biggest planet. It is mostly made of liquid. We know there is a big, red spot, which is a huge storm.

Jupiter ——————————————

**big, red spot**

This big, red spot is a storm as big
as some planets!

# Saturn

After Jupiter, we will see Saturn.

Saturn is another massive planet made mostly of liquid. Saturn has really big rings that are made of billions of chunks of ice.

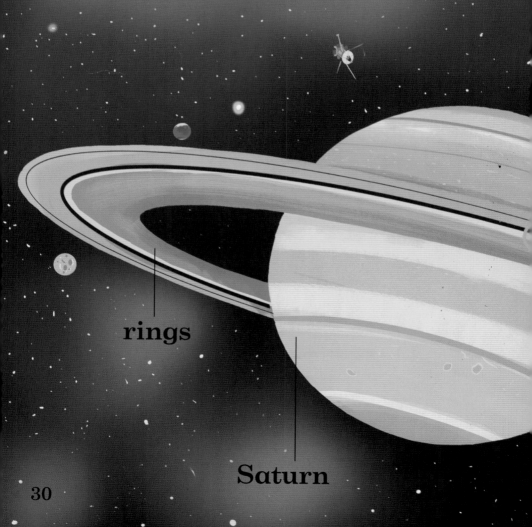

rings

Saturn

moons

Saturn also has many moons.
Moons orbit their planet.

# Uranus

The next planet our spacecraft will visit is Uranus.

Uranus is a massive, cold planet, which is mostly gas and liquid.

Uranus ————————

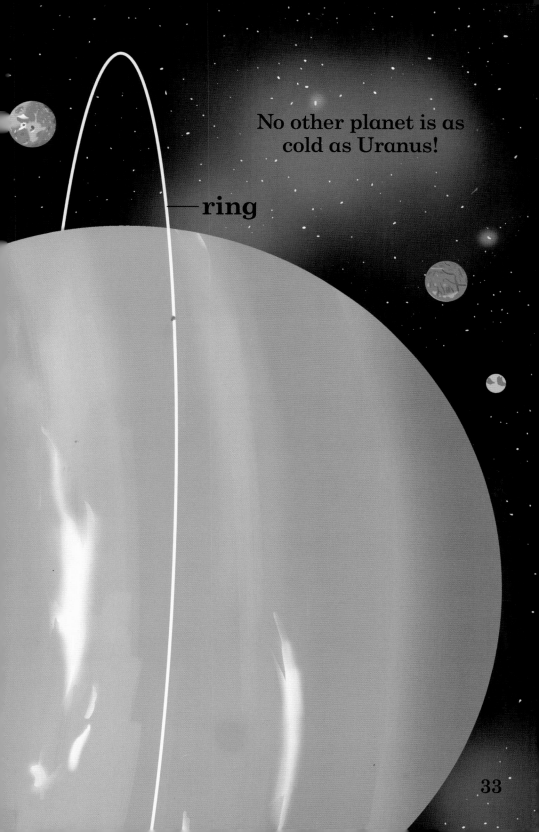

No other planet is as
cold as Uranus!

——ring

# Neptune

Next, our spacecraft
will go to Neptune.
Neptune is the last
of the massive planets
in our Solar System.
It has a big moon, Triton.

Neptune

Triton

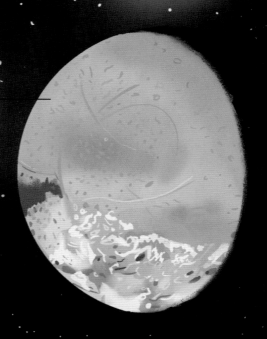

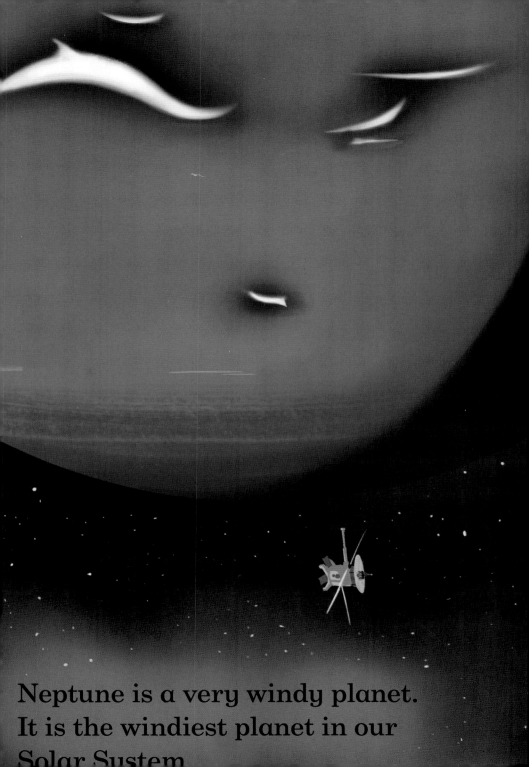

Neptune is a very windy planet. It is the windiest planet in our Solar System.

# Pluto

Now our spacecraft comes to the outside part of the Solar System.

We will see little Pluto before we go.

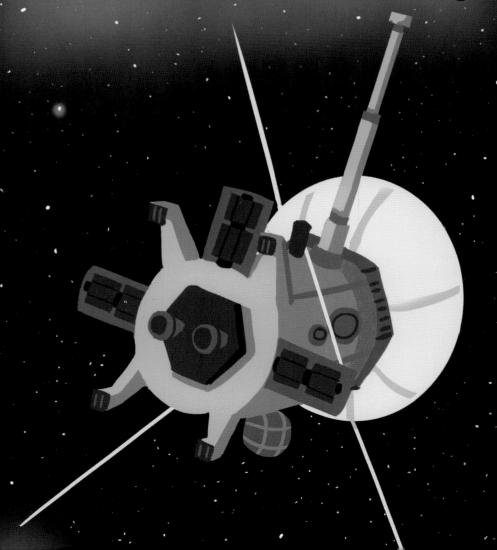

**Charon**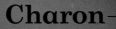

**Pluto**

Pluto is made of rock and ice and it is
very cold. Charon is Pluto's biggest moon.

# Dwarf planets

People used to call Pluto a planet.
But it is too little. Now people call
it a dwarf planet.

 Sun

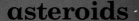 Pluto

asteroids

Pluto is just one of the dwarf planets
at the outside part of the Solar System.
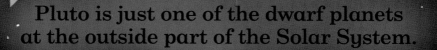

dwarf planets

There are icy asteroids here, too.

# Far, far away

We are coming to the very outside part of the Solar System.

From so far away, the Sun already looks like another star.

Sun

From far away, we can see how the Sun
is just like the billions of other stars.

# More solar systems

People now know that some other stars have solar systems, too.

Could things live there?

Other solar systems are much
too far away for people and their
robots to visit.

Imagine a spacecraft that could fly that far!

# Picture glossary

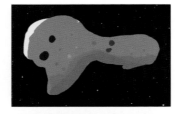 asteroid

 comet

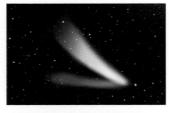 Earth

 Jupiter

 Mars

 Mercury

 Moon

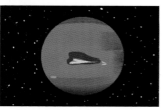 Neptune

 Saturn

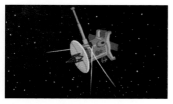 spacecraft

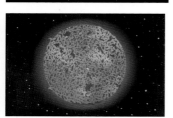 Sun

 Uranus

# Index

# Our Solar System quiz

What have you learnt about our Solar System? Answer these questions and find out!

- What is the name of the star in our Solar System?

- When is a comet's tail made?

- Where in our Solar System have people visited?

- Which is the biggest planet?

- What sort of planet is Pluto?

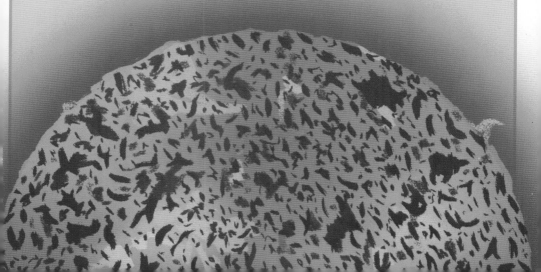

# Tick the books you've read!

## Level 3

Puss in Boots ☐
Sharks ☐
Thumbelina ☐
Aladdin ☐
YOU won't like this present as much as I DO! ☐

Jack and the Beanstalk ☐
Rapunzel ☐
The Jungle Book ☐
Hansel and Gretel ☐
The Elves and the Shoemaker ☐

Harry and the Bucketful of Dinosaurs ☐
The Red Knight ☐
Planet Earth ☐
Minibeasts ☐
SNAKE ATTACK! ☐

## Level 4

Dick Whittington ☐
Knights and Castles ☐
Peter and the Wolf ☐
Pinocchio ☐
I am Inventing an INVENTION ☐

The Pied Piper of Hamelin ☐
Snow White and the Seven Dwarfs ☐
The Wizard of Oz ☐
The Little Mermaid ☐
Alice in Wonderland ☐

Harry and the Dinosaurs United ☐
Heidi ☐
Our Solar System ☐
The Human Body ☐
FRIENDS STICK TOGETHER! ☐

 Available on the App Store

 ANDROID APP ON Google play

The Read it yourself with Ladybird app is now available